スクラップド・プリンセ
コンチェル
逃亡者達の協奏
SCRAPPED PRINCESS
3
Ichiro Sakaki
原作 榊一郎
Go Yabuki
作画 矢吹豪

Original work: Ichiro Sakaki

Original Character Design: Yukinobu Azumi

Illustrations: Go Yabuki

HAMBURG // LONDON // LOS ANGELES // TOKYO

Previously In

The epic sci-fi fantasy continues as the lives of everyone in the world hang in the balance! While Pacifica, Shannon and Raquel flee from bounty hunters, Pacifica crosses paths with a frightened girl who has a dark secret and a fatal wish. After the girl disappears, a mysterious pendant might hold the clue to saving her. The three siblings set off to find the girl, but when they finally locate her, she's not quite what she appears to be...

Scrapped Princess Vol. 3

Story: Ichiro Sakaki
Art: Go Yabuki
Character Plan: Yukinobu Azumi

Translation - Alethea Nibley
English Adaptation - Liesl M. Bradner
Retouch and Lettering - Fawn Lau
Production Artist - Alyson Stetz
Cover Design - Al-Insan Lashley

Editor - Julie Taylor
Digital Imaging Manager - Chris Buford
Managing Editor - Lindsey Johnston
VP of Production - Ron Klamert
Editor-In-Chief - Rob Tokar
Publisher - Mike Kiley
President and C.O.O. - John Parker
C.E.O. and Chief Creative Office - Stuart Levy

A  Manga

TOKYOPOP Inc.
5900 Wilshire Blvd. Suite 2000
Los Angeles, CA 90036

E-mail: info@TOKYOPOP.com
Come visit us online at www.TOKYOPOP.com

ISBN: 1-59532-983-8

First TOKYOPOP printing: May 2006

10 9 8 7 6 5 4 3 2 1

Printed in the USA

"OF THE TWINS WHICH SPRING FROM THE QUEEN'S WOMB..."
"SO SAYS THE 5111TH ORACLE OF ST. GRENDEL..."
"...YOU MUST KILL THE GIRL AT ONCE!"

Chapter Thirteen: The Oracle of Grendel Part One

"SHE WILL CREATE MOUNTAINS OF CORPSES AND RIVERS OF BLOOD."
"ON THE DAY APPOINTED BY DESTINY, SHE WILL BECOME THE POISON..."
"...THAT WILL DESTROY THE WORLD."
LET'S SEE...
THE RECORDS RELATING TO THE PROPHECY ...

15 YEARS AGO, THE FOUR PRIESTS CONNECTED TO THE ORACLE OF GRENDEL ALL PASSED AWAY.
IT IS SAID THAT THEIR DEATHS WERE CAUSED BY A CURSE, BUT NO ONE KNOWS FOR SURE.
AND THAT INCIDENT WAS HIDDEN AWAY BY BOTH THE ROYAL FAMILY AND THE CHURCH?
THE REATEST TABOO OF THE LINEVAN INGDOM.
"SCRAPPED PRINCESS," HUH? HEH HEH HEH! INTEREST-ING.

Chapter Thirteen: The Oracle of Grendel Part One

SHANNON-NII, YOU KNOW WHAT IT MEANS TO "TREAT" SOMEONE, RIGHT?
YEAH.
I DON'T THINK THIS WOULD BE CONSIDERED "TREATING" SOMEONE.

DON'T COMPLAIN!
THIS IS THE BEST WE CAN DO RIGHT NOW!!
IN OTHER WORDS, WE HAVE NO MONEY.

SO RIGHT NOW, EVEN *THIS* WOULD BE CONSIDERED A TREAT.
AW...

......
I'M NOT GIVING IT TO YOU.
?!

DO I LOOK LIKE A GREEDY PERSON, SHANNON-NII?!!
UNBELIEVABLE! JUST FOR THAT, YOU SHOULD GIVE ME YOUR SANDWICH!!
CALM DOWN.
HEY!
THAT'S MINE!!
BECAUSE OF THAT WOMAN, I... MY FAMILY...
MY FATHER DIED AT THE ORACLE OF GRENDEL...

MY MOTHER SAID HE WAS A FINE ORACLE--THAT HE SERVED GOD AND DIED AS A MARTYR. SO I SHOULD BE PROUD.

THE PEOPLE AROUND US WOULDN'T SEE IT THAT WAY. THE FAMILY OF ONE WHO MADE A CURSED PROPHECY... CURSED HUMANS.

WE'VE ALWAYS BEEN CALLED THAT.

IT'S ALL BECAUSE OF THE SCRAPPED PRINCESS.
IF ONLY THAT GIRL...
...HAD NEVER BEEN BORN.
...

SHANNON, IS SOMETHING WRONG?
......
NO, BUT SOMETHING IS BOTHERING ME.
WE SHOULD BE GOING.
YEAH.
AHHHH! OUR FIRST TOWN IN A LONG TIME.
WE'D BETTER FIND AN INN.

AN INN TO ME MEANS A MARBLE BATHTUB AND SOFT BEDS!

I TOLD YOU BEFORE...

...WE DON'T HAVE MUCH MONEY.

WHAT'S YOUR BUSINESS WITH US?
?
YOU ARE THE CAUSE OF ALL MY TROUBLES.
DAMN YOU, SCRAPPED PRINCESS!!

YOU KILLED MY FATHER! PREPARE YOURSELF!!

?!

W-WAIT! I DON'T KNOW WHAT YOU MEAN! I KILLED YOUR FATHER?!

UH!!
カッ
チ
ッ
ザッ
ザッ
UGH! WHAT'S WITH THIS GUY?!

RAQUEL!
MJOLLNIR, STRIKE!!
WALL, OBSTRUCT!!
DEFENSE MAGIC?!

THAT MAN CAN USE MAGIC TOO.
スッ
SO IT WOULD SEEM. AND HIS MARTIAL ARTS SKILLS ARE FIRST CLASS AS WELL.

IF I COULD JUST GET INSIDE THE RANGE OF HIS SPEAR...

IT'S SEGMENTED.

HEH HEH HEH.

IS THIS WHERE I SAY, "JUST WHAT WOULD I EXPECT OF HER GUARDIAN?"

WHO ARE YOU?! AND WHY ARE YOU SNEAKING AROUND AFTER US?
MY NAME IS RAGING BULL.
I AM A PAID MERCENARY.

TODAY IS JUST OUR WAY OF SAYING HELLO.

YOU HAVE A PRETTY DANGEROUS WAY OF GREETING PEOPLE.

MY EMPLOYER WOULD LIKE TO TALK TO YOU.

PACIFICA CASULL-- THE POISON THAT WILL DESTROY THE WORLD--THE SCRAPPED PRINCESS.

STARTING ON THIS DAY...

...WE WILL CONTINUE TO HUNT YOU, DAY AND NIGHT.
YOU SHALL PAY FOR THE CRIME OF KILLING MY FATHER.
WHILE THINKING ON THE MAGNITUDE OF DEATH AND DESTRUCTION YOU HAVE CAUSED...
...YOU WILL DIE, SUFFERING!!

SHE JUST DECIDES.

....
SHE'S DECLAR-ING WAR.

......
WE'VE RUN INTO SOME TROUBLE.
STILL...

YEAH.
PACIFICA.
JUST WONDERING WHAT ON EARTH THE "SCRAPPED PRINCESS" IS.
ARE YOU ALL RIGHT?
YOU WONDER THAT TOO, PACIFICA CASULL-SAN?
AAAHH, WAIT A MINUTE.
SHEESH! THEY JUST KEEP ON COMING.

I AM MILJITTE, A SCHOLAR OF NATURAL HISTORY.
SCHOLAR OF NATURAL HISTORY?
MIL-JITTE-SAN?!
Oh my! Pleased to meet you.
DO YOU KNOW HER?
NO.
I HAVE BEEN RESEARCHING THE ORACLES OF GRENDEL IN GENERAL, A UNIQUE CASE IN PARTICULAR.
IT'S ABOUT THE SCRAPPED PRINCESS.

I'VE BEEN RESEARCHING THE ORACLES OF GRENDEL.
AND I'VE FOUND I'M MOST INTERESTED IN THE ONE OF THE SCRAPPED PRINCESS.
!!
......

Chapter Fourteen: The Oracle of Grendel Part Two

Chapter Fourteen: The Oracle of Grendel Part Two

DOES THAT MEAN YOU'RE RESEARCHING ME?
THAT WOULD BE THE CASE.
FIRST OF ALL...
...RESEARCHING HER PROBABLY WON'T BENEFIT YOU IN ANY WAY.
I DON'T SENSE ANY HOSTILITY FROM THIS WOMAN, BUT...
...WE CAN'T LET OUR GUARD DOWN.
SO WHY ARE YOU HERE?
TO OBSERVE THE SCRAPPED PRINCESS!!

I DON'T THINK SO.
OHHH.
HEY, SHANNON.
WE DON'T KNOW MUCH ABOUT THE ORACLE, DO WE?
WELL... THAT IS TRUE, BUT...
SINCE SHE'S HERE, IS IT OKAY IF I ASK HER A QUESTION?
......
WHAT DO YOU THINK?
THAT GIRL SAID I KILLED HER FATHER.

DID I REALLY TAKE HIS LIFE?
I DON'T REMEMBER ANYTHING LIKE THAT!
?!
SCRAPPED PRINCESS...
IF I DID CAUSE HER FATHER'S DEATH, THEN...

...I CAN'T RUN AWAY FROM HER!!
MILJITTE-SAN?!
HEY, PACIFICA.
YOU SAID YOU'RE RESEARCHING ME, RIGHT?!
YES...

Hey...

IF YOU WANT TO OBSERVE ME, IT IS OKAY WITH ME.

OH MY! REALLY?!

......

Uh...

...IN EXCHANGE...

IF YOU WANT TO OBSERVE ME, YOU HAVE TO PAY FOR OUR ROOM AT AN INN!!

......

......
YOU DON'T KNOW ANYTHING ABOUT THE SCRAPPED PRINCESS, DO YOU?
HOW WOULD WE KNOW ABOUT THE LINEVAN KINGDOM'S GREATEST CURSE?
YOU'RE RIGHT.
WHERE WOULD YOU LIKE TO START, SCRAPPED PRINCESS-SAN?
IT'S PACIFICA.
DON'T CALL HER BY THAT NAME EVER AGAIN!!

ALL RIGHT.
UM, PACIFICA-SAN, WHAT WOULD YOU LIKE TO KNOW?
WELL...
TODAY, THERE WAS A GIRL WHO ATTACKED US AND SAID I KILLED HER FATHER.
BUT I DON'T KNOW WHAT SHE WAS TALKING ABOUT.
HMM.
THE GIRL WHO HIRED THAT RAGING BULL, RIGHT?

I WAS WATCHING.
S-SERIOUSLY?
YOU KNOW ABOUT HER?!
WELL, I HAD HEARD ABOUT HER VIA SOME INFORMATION I GOT FROM UNOFFICIAL SOURCES.
YES.
SHE IS THE DAUGHTER OF A PRIEST WHO DIED AT THE ORACLE OF GRENDEL, AND SHE'S HIRED A MERCENARY TO KILL YOU.
UNOFFICIAL SOURCES, HUH?
OH MY. INFORMATION CAN BE THE GREATEST WEAPON, YOU KNOW?! YOU HAVE TO CONSIDER BOTH OFFICIAL AND UNDERGROUND SOURCES PROPERLY.
MIL-JITTE-SAN, YOU SAID HE DIED AT THE ORACLE OF GRENDEL?

WHEN THE PROPHECY WAS GIVEN, THE FOUR PRIESTS WHO RECEIVED IT ALL MET WITH MYSTERIOUS DEATHS.

IF YOU LOOK AT IT FROM THAT GIRL'S POINT OF VIEW, I SUPPOSE YOU COULD SAY THAT HER FATHER DIED IN ORDER TO TELL OF THE EXISTENCE OF THE SCRAPPED PRINCESS.

BUT THERE IS MORE TO IT.

THE FAMILIES OF THE PRIESTS ARE ALL FOLLOWING PATHS OF MISFORTUNE.

THE PROPHECY ITSELF WASN'T MADE TABOO, SO THE PEOPLE WHO DON'T KNOW THE CIRCUMSTANCES AVOID THEM AS "THE FAMILIES OF THE PRIESTS WHO MYSTERIOUSLY DISAPPEARED."

AND THOSE WHO DO KNOW AVOID THEM AS "THE FAMILIES OF THOSE WHO GAVE A HORRIFYING PROPHECY."

IT'S ONLY MY THEORY, THOUGH.

WHAT'S WRONG?

I'M GETTING A LITTLE CONFUSED, SO I'M GOING OUTSIDE TO REST.

OH.

YOU KILLED MY FATHER!!
THE FAMILIES OF THOSE WHO GAVE A HORRIFYING PROPHECY...
BECAUSE OF ME...
WHAT'S WRONG, PACIFICA?
?!
Oof!
SHAN-NON-NII!
GEEZ! DID YOU HAVE TO CLIMB ALL THE WAY UP TO THE ROOF?
SHUT UP!
IT'S NOT LIKE IT MAT-TERS!

HEY, SHANNON-NII...
I WONDER IF MAYBE I...REALLY SHOULDN'T HAVE BEEN BORN.
EVERYONE IS SO UNHAPPY BECAUSE OF ME.
EVEN YOU AND RAQUEL-NEE.
ARE YOU SAYING THAT STUFF AGAIN?!
HEY!

ALL THAT STUFF WITH THE ORACLE HAPPENED BEFORE YOU WERE BORN.
YOU DIDN'T CHOOSE ANY OF THIS, SO DON'T MAKE IT YOUR FAULT.
BESIDES... IF IT IS A CURSE...
...RAQUEL AND I WOULD HAVE DIED LONG AGO.
SO ARE YOU SAYING THAT WHEN YOU FOUND OUT I WAS THE SCRAPPED PRINCESS...
...YOU WEREN'T SCARED?

WELL... YOU ARE WHAT YOU ARE.
WHAT'S THAT?!!
PFT.
WH- WHAT?!
WELL... YOU KNOW.
I CAN'T SAY I WASN'T...
EH?
BUT...
YOU *ARE* THE SCRAPPED PRINCESS.

THAT YOU MIGHT DISAPPEAR FROM OUR LIVES...*THAT* IS WHAT I WAS SCARED OF.

SOMETHING LIKE THAT.

YEAH.

THANKS,
SHANNON-NII.

RAGING BULL!
I RESTRAINED MYSELF BACK THERE, JUST LIKE YOU TOLD ME TO.
IS THERE A PROBLEM, TARSA?
YES! OF COURSE THERE IS!
I FINALLY FOUND HER!!

WHAT IF SHE GETS AWAY? NO-- WHAT IF SOMEONE ELSE KILLS HER FIRST?
I WANT TO KILL THE SCRAPPED PRINCESS WITH MY OWN HANDS!!
......

ARE YOU...
...PREPARED?!
DO YOU UNDERSTAND WHAT IT MEANS TO KILL SOMEONE?
ARE YOU PREPARED TO BEAR THAT BURDEN?!
ARE YOU HONESTLY READY FOR THAT?

ARE ...

ARE YOU SAYING THE SCRAPPED PRINCESS IS HUMAN? YOU'RE JOKING!!

SHE LOOKED LIKE A NORMAL HUMAN BEING TO ME. DID YOU NOT SEE THAT?

COULD YOU NOT SEE PAST THE STIGMA OF THE "SCRAPPED PRINCESS"?

DID YOU NOT SEE A THINKING, FEELING, LIVING, REAL PERSON?

HUMAN? THE SCRAPPED PRINCESS?!

I'LL ASK YOU AGAIN--ARE YOU PREPARED TO KILL ANOTHER HUMAN BEING?
THE BEING THAT SHOULD BE DETESTED.
THE SCRAPPED PRINCESS.
MY ENEMY, WHOM I THOUGHT TO BE THE POISON THAT WOULD DESTROY THE WORLD.
JUST A HUMAN...?
PEOPLE HAVE DIED.

TO KILL...
...ANOTHER PERSON.
I'M GOING TO...
...KILL THAT GIRL?!
ブル
ブル

KILLING A PERSON...
ARE YOU PRE-PARED FOR THAT?
I'M GOING TO KILL THAT GIRL.
PERHAPS THE SCRAPPED PRINCESS IS HUMAN.

Chapter Fifteen: The Oracle of Grendel Part Three

Chapter Fifteen: The Oracle of Grendel Part Three

SEARCH EVERY-WHERE!!
WE HAVE WITNES-SES!!
FOR OUR LORD MAUSER AND THE LINEVAN KINGDOM, WE MUST DESTROY THE SCRAPPED PRINCESS!!
WHAT?
FOR THEIR LORD MAUSER AND THE KINGDOM, HUH?
THAT WAS CLOSE.

WE HAVE TO BE GRATEFUL TO MILJITTE-SAN.

YEAH, IF SHE HADN'T WARNED US...
FOR SOME REASON I HATE THAT GUY GIVING ORDERS.

THEY SAY HE'S THE FEUDAL LORD HERE AND A FOLLOWER OF THE MAUSER FAITH.
BUT HE DOESN'T SEEM TO HAVE A VERY GOOD REPUTATION.

HE PROBABLY JUST WANTS SOME NOTORIETY.

THE TOWN GATES ARE COMPLETELY BLOCKED.
IT WON'T BE EASY FOR US TO GET OUT OF HERE.

YOU'RE RIGHT.
BUT WE CAN'T STAY HERE FOREVER, EITHER.

MAN! THIS HAS GOTTEN TO BE A PAIN.

WE'VE GOT ENOUGH TROUBLE WITH THE PUNITIVE FORCE.

NOW WE HAVE TO...
...TAKE **THEM** ON TOO?

I GUESS NOT ALL OF THE PEOPLE WHO ARE AFTER PACIFICA...

...ARE DOING IT BECAUSE OF THEIR BELIEF IN THE PROPHECY.

YOU KILLED MY FATHER. PREPARE YOURSELF!!

IT'S CRAZY.

SHE'S THE ONE SUFFERING THE MOST.

UNTIL NOW, "SCRAPPED PRINCESS" WAS JUST A NAME.
BUT SHE CERTAINLY WAS HUMAN.
THE MOMENT I REALIZED MY OPPONENT WAS HUMAN...
...I STARTED TO HESITATE.
I WONDER IF... THE MOMENT I KILL THE SCRAPPED PRINCESS, WHO KILLED MY FATHER, IF I MIGHT...
...BECOME JUST LIKE THE SCRAPPED PRINCESS?
THAT WAY!
?

I WONDER WHAT'S GOING ON.
THAT'S STRANGE.
YOU FOUND THE SCRAPPED PRINCESS? GOOD.
GATHER THE SOLDIERS IMMEDIATE-- HMM?
WELL, WELL.
IF IT ISN'T TARSA-DONO.

YOU'D BETTER LEAVE THIS PLACE QUICKLY.

WHAT WAS THAT?

THIS ISN'T A PLACE SOMEONE SO TAINTED SHOULD BEFOUL.

DON'T LOOK SO ANGRY.

I'M GOING TO GO KILL THE SCRAPPED PRINCESS AND AVENGE YOUR FATHER.

AND MY DOING SO SHOULD CLEANSE A LITTLE OF YOUR FILTH.
?!
IT'S TRUE THAT IF I LEAVE IT TO THE SOLDIERS, THEN I WON'T HAVE TO GET DIRECTLY INVOLVED.
BUT IF THE SCRAPPED PRINCESS IS KILLED BY THE PUNITIVE FORCE...

...WILL I BE ABLE TO GET CLOSURE FOR MY OWN FEELINGS?
ALL THE SUFFERING I'VE GONE THROUGH...
...AND THE HATRED...WILL ALL BECOME MEANINGLESS.
IF THAT HAPPENS...
...THEN WHAT ON EARTH...

WHAT ON EARTH WILL I HAVE LEFT?!

RAGING BULL...

I'M GOING TO STOP THEM.

YOU UNDERSTAND THAT YOU'LL BECOME A FUGITIVE, TOO.

YEAH, I KNOW.

BUT IF THE SCRAPPED PRINCESS WAS KILLED BY ANYONE OTHER THAN ME...
...I COULDN'T STAND IT!!
I SEE.
IN THAT CASE ....
LET'S GO!!
YES!

YOU ENJOY CHASING AFTER DELICATE, BEAUTIFUL YOUNG WOMEN?!
SHAMELESS COWARDS!!
MAN! WHAT GOOD WILL IT DO TO PROVOKE THE ENEMY WHILE RUNNING AWAY?
WELL ...
THERE THEY ARE!!

DON'T LET THEM ESCAPE!
AH...
THERE'S NO END TO THEM.

WE'LL GET TO THE GATE SOON! RUN AS FAST AS YOU CAN!!
Haa
Haa
OKAY!!
WALL...
...OBSTRUCT!
?!
I THINK I MESSED UP.
Haa
This is a problem.
SHANNON-NII, ISN'T THIS...

...WHAT THEY CALL "HAVING YOUR BACK AGAINST THE WALL"?

WELL... TYPICALLY, YEAH.
IT'S OKAY, PACIFICA. WE'RE NOT TYPICAL PEOPLE.
YEAH. THAT SUCKS.

WE'VE FINALLY CORNERED YOU, SCRAPPED PRINCESS AND GUARDIANS.
THERE'S NOWHERE LEFT TO RUN!!
Ha ha...
FILTHY BEINGS. I SHALL CLEANSE YOU.
AAAHH! I REALLY DO HATE HIM.
PACIFICA, DON'T LEAVE MY SIDE, OKAY?
GET THEM!!

THEY'RE BEHIND US TOO?!

THERE'RE JUST TOO MANY.

I HAVE TO FIND A WAY OUT.

PACIFICA, BEHIND YOU!!
?!
CRAP!!

?!
YOU?!

Chapter Sixteen: The Oracle of Grendel Part Four

ザッ
ヒュッ
ガッ

Chapter Sixteen: The Oracle of Grendel Part Four

DAMMIT! BECAUSE OF THOSE TWO, MY PLANS TO DESTROY THE SCRAPPED PRINCESS ARE AT RISK!
BUT THE SOLDIERS OUTNUMBER THEM.
?!
TARSA.
SO THAT WOMAN REALLY IS...
HEY! GIVE ME YOUR BOW!!

LOOK
OUT!!

?!
NOW! CAPTURE HER!!
PACIFICA?!

PACIFICA!!
?!

SHANNON-NII!!

HA HA HA! GOOD WORK!! YOU TOOK DOWN ONE OF THE GUARDIANS!!

KILL THE OTHERS! BUT DON'T KILL THE SCRAPPED PRINCESS OR TARSA!!

SHANNON-NII!!

PACI-
FICA!
UH.
HEY,
DON'T
MOVE!!
LET GO!
SHANNON-
NII!!

HMMM.

YOU'RE FINALLY AWAKE.
......
WHERE ARE WE?

IN JAIL, SCRAPPED PRINCESS.

HUH?
WE'VE BEEN CAPTURED BY THE FEUDAL LORD.
UUUGH!
......
AAARGH!
WHAT IS THIS?!!
HOW DO I GET THESE OFF?
WHAT ARE YOU DOING?
WELL, IF WE CAN'T GET THEM OFF, WE CAN'T ESCAPE.
IF THEY CAME OFF THAT EASILY...
...I WOULD HAVE TAKEN MINE OFF AND KILLED YOU LONG AGO!

HA HA
HA HA...
がっくし
......
チラ
SHEESH.
WHAT ON EARTH IS SHE THINKING?
ガチャ
ガチャ
SAY, SCRAPPED PRINCESS...

HMPH!
I REALLY DON'T LIKE BEING CALLED THAT!
....
PACIFICA CASULL. HOW'S THAT?
YOU *DO* KNOW MY NAME.
I'D NEVER FORGET THE NAME OF SOMEONE I SHOULD HATE.
BESIDES, I'M GOING TO KILL YOU.

SO WHY...
...DID YOU HELP ME, BACK THEN?
....
YOU HELPED ME TOO. DIDN'T YOU?

THAT'S BECAUSE I DIDN'T WANT THAT FEUDAL LORD TO GET TO YOU BEFORE I DID!!
I...
...I WOULD HATE IT...
...FOR MORE PEOPLE TO SUFFER BECAUSE OF THEIR CONNECTION TO ME.
I DON'T WANT...
...ANY MORE PEOPLE TO DIE.

THAT'S ALL.
......
ガチャッ
TERRIBLY SORRY TO INTERRUPT.
SCRAPPED PRINCESS...
...YOUR PUBLIC EXECUTION HAS BEEN SET FOR TODAY.
AND I HAVE COME TO RETRIEVE YOU.
TODAY, THE WICKED BEING KNOWN AS THE SCRAPPED PRINCESS WILL BE PURGED.
WHAT DID YOU SAY?

GO AHEAD AND TRY!
I'LL SHOW YOU THE HIDDEN POWERS OF THIS SWEET, DELICATE, SUPER GIRL!!!
I'LL PUNCH YOU RIGHT IN THE FACE!!
SILENCE!!
THERE WILL BE ONE MORE PUBLIC EXECUTION. THAT OF THE ONE WHO HAS AIDED THE SCRAPPED PRINCESS-- TARSA.
HEH HEH HEH. SUCH A FITTING DEATH FOR YOU, TARSA.
THIS IS FOR THE SAKE OF OUR OLD FRIENDSHIP. YOU SHOULD BE GRATEFUL.

FOR THE SAKE OF OLD FRIENDSHIP, HUH?
BEFORE THE PROPHECY, OUR FAMILIES WERE FRIENDS.
BUT AFTER THE PROPHECY, YOU HID THAT FACT.
AND WHEN MY MOTHER AND I CAME TO YOU FOR HELP, YOU HAD US EXILED.
IN THE END, YOU SAW US AS THINGS.
AS TOOLS TO IMPROVE YOUR REPUTATION AND SOCIAL STANDING.

IF RAGING BULL HADN'T SAID ANYTHING TO ME BACK THEN...
...I MIGHT HAVE THOUGHT THE SAME WAY AS THIS MAN.
EXCUSE ME!

YOU DO SOME PRETTY TERRIBLE THINGS!!
EVEN IF THEY DID HAVE SOMETHING TO DO WITH THE PROPHECY, THOSE WERE HER PARENTS, RIGHT?
SHE HERSELF HAD NOTHING TO DO WITH IT!!
WHY DO YOU HOLD THAT AGAINST HER?!
YOU DON'T KNOW?

ABSOLUTE PROPHECIES. AMONG THEM, THE WORST OF THE WORST IS THE ORACLE OF THE SCRAPPED PRINCESS.
LOOK, YOU!
HOW CAN I TREAT THE DAUGHTER OF THE ONE WHO MADE SUCH A PROPHECY AS A NORMAL PERSON?
STOP SAYING SUCH SELFISH THINGS! DON'T YOU CARE THE TINIEST BIT ABOUT PEOPLE'S PAIN?!

WHO WOULD PROPHESY SUCH A THING JUST BECAUSE THEY WANTED TO?!
I'M THE ONE YOU WANT, SO LEAVE HER ALONE!
....
I DON'T CARE ABOUT ANY OF THAT.
JUST AS TARSA SAID, YOU BOTH ARE NOTHING MORE THAN TOOLS TO BUILD MY REPUTATION.
IT'S ALMOST TIME.
YES.
HEY!

WHAT'S HAPPENED TO SHANNON-NII AND RAQUEL-NEE?
WE'RE SEARCHING FOR YOUR SISTER AND TARSA'S BODYGUARD. IT'S ONLY A MATTER OF TIME.
AS FOR YOUR BROTHER...
...HIS BODY HASN'T SURFACED, BUT HE'S PROBABLY DEAD.
YOU'RE LYING! SHANNON-NII CAN'T BE DEAD!!
YOU'RE STILL WORRIED ABOUT OTHERS AT A TIME LIKE THIS?
HMM! YOU CAN BELIEVE WHATEVER YOU WANT.

SHANNON-
NII!!!

THIS EVENING, WE WILL HOLD THE LONG-AWAITED PUBLIC EXECUTION.
Chapter Fifteen: The Oracle of Grendel Part Five
HEE HEE HEE.
SHANNON-NII...

SHAN-NON...
I SEE YOU'RE AWAKE.
I'M BACK.
UH!
AAAHH! YOU MUSTN'T MOVE.
SHE'S RIGHT. YOU SHOULD RELAX.
YOU...
YOU HELPED US?

IT LOOKS LIKE YOU'RE AWAKE.

HE'S THE ONE THAT HELPED YOU.

RAGING BULL! WHY DID YOU HELP ME?!

YOUR LITTLE SISTER HELPED MY CLIENT. ALL I DID WAS REPAY THE DEBT.

WHEN YOU FELL IN THE RIVER, HE JUMPED IN AND SAVED YOU.

THAT WASN'T MY BEST MOMENT. BUT HOW DID YOU GET ME OUT?!

WHERE'S PACIFICA?!

......

SHE'S BEEN CAPTURED.

AND THEY ARE EXECUTING HER TONIGHT.

RAQUEL!!

......

I GUESS IT'S USELESS TO STOP YOU...

YEAH.

NOW HOLD ON.

YOU'RE GOING TOO, AREN'T YOU?

OF COURSE.

I WOULD BE A DISGRACE AS A SOLDIER IF I ABANDONED MY EMPLOYER.

THAT MAKES THINGS EASIER.

I HAVE A PLAN.

I COULDN'T ACCOMPLISH ANYTHING. I COULDN'T CHANGE ANYTHING.
IT'S GOING TO END LIKE THIS.
AND THE PERSON I SHOULD HAVE KILLED...
...WAS TAKEN BY THAT GUY.

?!
WHY IS SHE--?
I DON'T UNDER-STAND.
WHAT'S THE DIFFERENCE BETWEEN HER AND ME?

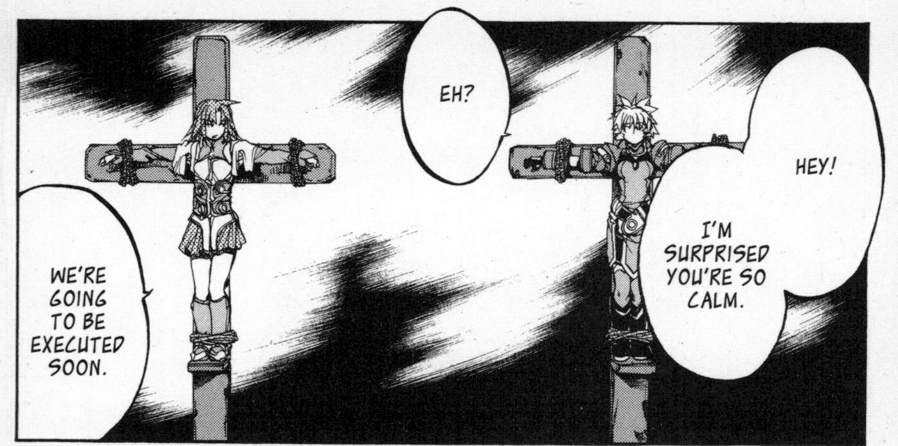
HEY!
I'M SURPRISED YOU'RE SO CALM.
EH?
WE'RE GOING TO BE EXECUTED SOON.

......?
YOU'RE NOT SCARED?
DO I LOOK LIKE I'M NOT SCARED?
WELL, I *AM* SCARED!

IF I LOOK LIKE I'M CALM...
...I GUESS IT'S BECAUSE I'VE GOTTEN USED TO PEOPLE WANTING TO KILL ME.
OR...
...I'M THINKING THAT I ABSOLUTELY CAN'T DIE. ONE OR THE OTHER.

……
IF ONLY I HAD SUCH…
ABSO-LUTELY CAN'T DIE.
LADIES AND GENTLEMEN!
WE WILL NOW BEGIN THE PUBLIC EXECUTION.

TO DEMONSTRATE MY FAITH IN THE MAUSER CHURCH...
...I, THE FEUDAL LORD, WILL PERFORM THE EXECUTION MYSELF.
......
I TOLD YOU!
DON'T MAKE ME SAY IT AGAIN!!

YOU NARCISSISTIC PSYCHO!!
WHA--!
THERE ARE ONLY TWO PEOPLE IN THE WORLD...
...WHO ARE ALLOWED TO KILL ME.

?!
AND YOU'RE NOT ONE OF THEM!
AARGH!

HOW DARE YOU MOCK ME!
I'M BEGINNING THE EXECUTION! BRING ME A SPEAR!!
YES, SIR!

WHA-WHAT'S GOING ON?!
YOU'VE BEEN BULLYING MY LITTLE SISTER, HAVEN'T YOU?
IF YOU LAY A HAND ON HER AGAIN... I WON'T BE ABLE TO FORGIVE YOU!!
RAQUEL-NEE!!
I'M SORRY I'M LATE, PACIFICA.
WHAT IS THAT?
WHAT'S GOING ON?

A-ATTACK MAGIC!!
IF WE DON'T GET AWAY, IT'LL GET US TOO!!
WAAHH!
RUN!!
WE'LL BE KILLED!!
ALL OF YOU! STOP!!
THE SCRAPPED PRINCESS! HAVE THE SOLDIERS SEIZE HER!!
I-IT'S NO USE. WE'LL GET SWEPT UP IN THE CROWD.
THEN KILL HER!!
SHANNON-NII!!

LOOK, YOU... WHAT GOOD WILL IT DO TO MAKE THEM ANGRY?
HUH?
AH! SHANNON-NII!
YEAH ...
WHAT TOOK YOU SO LONG?
STOP! WHAT ARE YOU DOING? I'M INJURED!!
AH... SHANNON-NII, WHAT ABOUT YOUR INJURIES?
IT'S A LITTLE LATE TO WORRY NOW.

LORD THAT BURNS THE HEAVENS, CLAD IN PALE LIGHTNING...
MASTER OF THE RAGING THUNDER...
ROARING ONE...
COME FORTH, SUUPII-KUN!!
ELECTRIFY THEM!
GO!
WHAT ARE THESE THINGS?!!
WAAAAAHH!

UGH. D-DAMN YOU, SCRAPPED PRINCESS.
I TOLD YOU BEFORE...

THE ONLY ONES ALLOWED TO KILL ME...ARE SHANNON-NII AND RAQUEL-NEE!!

ARE THEY DEAD?
NO.
THEY'VE JUST FAINTED FROM SHOCK.
THEY PROBABLY WON'T BE ABLE TO MOVE FOR A WHILE.
ゴッ
I SEE...

WHAT WILL YOU DO? WILL YOU SETTLE THINGS HERE?!
THAT ALL DEPENDS ON YOU.

I THINK THAT I ABSOLUTELY CAN'T DIE.
THE REASON SHE CAN'T DIE...
THE ONLY ONES ALLOWED TO KILL ME ARE SHANNON-NII AND RAQUEL-NEE!
...IS HER PREPAREDNESS TO BE KILLED.
IT'S ALL FOCUSED ON HER.
ASIDE FROM KILLING HER, WHAT'S LEFT FOR ME?
Chapter Sixteen: The Oracle of Grendel Part Si

OH...
Chapter Sixteen: The Oracle of Grendel Part Six

I SEE IT HAS BEGUN.

I HAVE LIVED FOR THIS DAY, SO THAT I COULD KILL YOU.
YOU ARE THE CAUSE OF MY FATHER'S DEATH. IT IS BECAUSE OF YOU THAT THINGS HAVE TURNED OUT LIKE THIS.

......

IF I HADN'T BEEN BORN, YOUR FAMILY WOULDN'T HAVE SUFFERED.

HOW CAN YOU ACCEPT IT SO CALMLY?!!

AS IF YOU KNOW WHAT I'VE BEEN THROUGH!
HOW CAN YOU SAY SUCH THINGS?!

I UNDERSTAND! I KNOW HOW YOU FEEL!!

HOW COULD YOU *POSSIBLY* UNDERSTAND?!!

?!
PACIFICA!!
UUH!

RAQUEL, HELP PACIFICA!!

I WON'T LET YOU!

PEOPLE OF FLAME, DANCE!

WALL, OB-STRUCT.

HE'S STRONG. HE'S A TOUGH MATCH EVEN WHEN I'M PAIRED WITH RAQUEL.
HUFF
HUFF

I DO UNDER-STAND.
I DO UNDER-STAND...
...HAVING ONE'S EXISTENCE CURSED.
HAVING THE WHOLE WORLD AGAINST YOU.
HAVING YOUR DESTINY DECIDED BY AN ORACLE.
SHUT UP!!
I-I'M THE SAME AS YOU.

I KNOW I'M THE CAUSE OF A LOT OF UNHAPPINESS.

AND THAT IT MIGHT HAVE BEEN A SIN TO BE BORN.

BUT EVEN SO...

...EVEN SO--I CAN'T DIE!!

SHANNON-NII AND RAQUEL-NEE GAVE UP EVERYTHING TO PROTECT ME.
I... HAVE A FAMILY THAT CARES FOR ME.
THAT'S WHY I CAN'T AFFORD TO DIE!!

YOU CAN SAY THOSE THINGS BECAUSE YOU HAVE A FAMILY!
I DON'T HAVE ANY FAMILY ANYMORE!!
CUT THE CRAP!!
YOU!
YOU'RE JUST BLAMING ALL YOUR PROBLEMS AND UNHAPPINESS ON PACIFICA!

YOU JUST CAN'T ACCEPT YOUR OWN MISFORTUNE!!
SHUT UP!
PARDON ME FOR LISTENING IN.
BUT IT'S LIKE SHANNON SAYS.
WHEN YOU BRING THAT DAGGER DOWN...
...WILL IT MAKE A DIFFERENCE?
WILL IT REALLY MAKE YOU HAPPY?

IF IT DOESN'T...
...HOW WILL YOU LIVE WITH YOURSELF AFTER THAT?

I'M NO GOOD AT THAT KIND OF THING. IT MAKES ME TIRED.

......
THAT'S A LIE. IT'S MUCH EASIER TO BLAME SOMEONE ELSE.
HOW IS SHE ABLE TO BE SO STRONG?
YOU REALLY...
...YOU REALLY ARE STRONG.
I CAN'T BE THAT STRONG.

I'M WEAK. I UNDERSTAND THAT MYSELF.
BUT I'M NOT ALONE.
I HAVE SHANNON-NII AND RAQUEL-NEE.

BUT...
チャ
I HAVE NOTHING LEFT.
I CAN'T BE LIKE YOU.
スッ
?!

グググッ

STUPID! WHY ARE YOU GIVING UP SO EASILY?!!
......
IF YOU DIE, IT'S ALL OVER!!

ガチッ
IF YOU DIE, YOU'LL LOSE EVERY-THING.
IF YOU GIVE UP, THAT'S THE END.
PLEASE! I DON'T THINK YOU REALLY WANT TO DIE.

WELL... WE'RE OFF.
YEAH.
I'M SORRY FOR CAUSING YOU SO MUCH TROUBLE.
UH-HUH. I'M SORRY, TOO.
IF WE EVER MEET AGAIN...

...I HOPE I CAN SHOW YOU A DIFFERENT SIDE OF ME.

YEAH.

IT'S A PROMISE.

SAY, RAGING BULL.
?
I WONDER IF I CAN BE STRONG.
コクッ
IT'S NOT LIKE EVERYONE STARTS OUT STRONG.
THOSE WHO DON'T KNOW THEIR OWN WEAKNESS CAN'T BECOME STRONG.
THAT'S EXACTLY WHY...

...WITHOUT A DOUBT, TOMORROW YOU WILL BE STRONGER THAN YOU HAVE BEEN TODAY.
THANKS.
HMM...
YOU'VE GOTTEN TO HAVE GOOD EYES.

MILJITTE-SAN'S LEFT TOO, HUH?
YEAH.
IT'S ALL RIGHT. HAVE FAITH.
YOU THREE WILL BE THE THIRD TIME*.
THAT GOES WITHOUT SAYING.
YEAH.

he past, the Oracle of Grendel has only been wrong twice.

LET'S BE THE THIRD TIME.
YEAH.

THERE ARE TIMES WHEN, AFTER BEING TOLD, "YOU ARE THE SCRAPPED PRINCESS," I WONDERED IF THAT WAS REALLY THE TRUTH.
EPILOGUE
AND THERE ARE TIMES WHEN I WONDERED, AFTER BEING TOLD I SHOULD BE HATED, IF THAT WAS TRUE TOO.
TO BE HONEST...I DON'T BELIEVE ANY OF IT.

BUT WHEN I HEAR ABOUT THE MISFORTUNE THAT HAPPENS TO PEOPLE CONNECTED TO ME...
...I FEEL LIKE MY HEART IS BREAKING.
MAYBE IT'S LIKE THE MAUSER CHURCH SAYS.
MAYBE THINGS WOULD BE BETTER IF I'D NEVER BEEN BORN.

THEN NO ONE WOULD BE UNHAPPY ANYMORE.
IT MIGHT BE EASIER THAT WAY.
WE...
...WILL PROTECT YOU!
BUT...
...THERE ARE PEOPLE...
...WHO BELIEVE IN ME ENOUGH TO RISK THEIR OWN LIVES.

PEOPLE WHO SAW THE REAL ME.
SHANNON-NII, RAQUEL-NEE...

...AND SO MANY PEOPLE WE'VE MET IN OUR TRAVELS.
THAT'S WHY I THINK I'LL JUST BE ME.

ACCEPTING EVERYTHING, EVEN THAT I'M THE SCRAPPED PRINCESS.
I WANT TO BE PACIFICA CASULL.
HEY! YOU AWAKE?
WHAT?
WE'VE ALMOST MADE IT TO TOWN.
I WILL NEVER GIVE UP ON LIVING.
TOWN! THEY'LL HAVE EGGS, RIGHT, SHANNON-NII?!!
LOOK, YOU. DON'T BE SUCH A GLUTTON ALL THE TIME.
HOW RUDE! FIRST OF ALL, SHANNON-NII, YOU...
Scrapped Princess: End

To those of you I've never met, pleased to meet you! To those of you I have met, it's been a long time! This is Yabuki.

The manga version of "Scrapped Princess" has reached its third and final volume. It's been about a year and a half, I suppose.
Thanks to all of you readers that have been able to get this far.
The series has also ended without incident.
I truly thank you.
I truly have been able to learn many things from this series.

Also, using this page, I would like to express my apologies and my gratitude.
First, I apologize...
Now that the series is over, I have realized again how truly inadequate I am.
I want to be able to be more diligent in creating something that all of my readers can be more satisfied in.
And my gratitude...
I'm glad that I was able to work to the end with such a helpful and talented staff and my editor I-san.
And to the creator, Sakaki-sensei, thank you for giving me the opportunity to work on such a wonderful series, despite my inadequacies.
And finally, a big thank you to all of the readers...

I would be very happy if we could meet again in another series someday.

2003.12.16 矢吹豪

Manga...

...after~
word.

I LOOK OVER MY OWN WORK AGAIN.

I READ OVER THE ORIGINAL WORK AGAIN.

AND I LEARN HOW TRULY INADEQUATE I AM.
Sute-Pri*

I LEARNED MANY THINGS FROM SUTE-PRI.
I WOULD LIKE TO BE ABLE TO DO BETTER THAN I EVER HAVE AND MEET EVERYONE AGAIN IN ANOTHER SERIES.

*Short for "suteta purinsesu" (Scrapped Princess)

SCRAPPED PRINCESS

榊 一郎 *Ichiro Sakaki*

矢吹 豪 *Go Yabuki*

staff

たらさわきょうこ *Kyoko Tarasawa*

安田正道 *Masamichi Yasuda*

矢野利憲 *Toshinori Yano*

special thanks

僕 牧人 *Boku Makito*

外山太一 *Taichi Toyama*

that I'm not like other people...

BIZENGHAST

When a young girl moves to the forgotten town of Bizenghast, she uncovers a terrifying collection of lost souls that leads her to the brink of insanity. One thing becomes painfully clear: The residents of Bizenghast are just dying to come home.

SHRINE OF THE MORNING MIST

BY HIROKI UGAWA

When the spirit world suddenly shifts out of balance, it's up to sisters Kurako, Yuzu and Tama to save us—but first they must get through their family drama.

FANTASY | TEEN AGE 13+

CONFIDENTIAL CONFESSIONS -DEAI-

BY REIKO MOMOCHI

In this unflinching portrayal of teens in crisis, silence isn't always golden...

DEATH JAM

BY JEON SANG YOUNG

Muchaca Smooth is an assassin with just one shot to make it big!

ROZEN MAIDEN

BY PEACH-PIT

Welcome to the world of *Rozen Maiden* where a boy must enter an all-new reality to protect and serve a living doll!

From the creators of *DearS*!

BOYS OF SUMMER

BY CHUCK AUSTEN AND HIROKI OTSUKA

Just because you strike out on your first attempt at scoring with a girl doesn't mean you won't end up hitting a home run!

KAT & MOUSE

BY ALEX DE CAMPI AND FEDERICA MANFREDI

When science whiz Kat teams up with computer nerd Mouse, bullies and blackmailers don't stand a chance!